Monster meat eaters!

This book belongs to

....

Beware!

This Really Creepy-Crawly Reader
comes complete with its own

monster
meat eater!

Check out page 12 to find out why
the centipede is a gruesome hunter.

Monster meat eaters!

make believe ideas

Reading together

This book is an ideal first reader for your child, combining simple words and sentences with stunning color photography. Here are some of the many ways you can help your child take those first steps in reading. Encourage your child to:

- Look at and explore the detail in the pictures.

- Sound out the letters in each word.

- Read and repeat each short sentence.

Look at the pictures

Make the most of each page by talking about the pictures and finding key words. Here are some questions you can use to discuss each page as you go along:

- Does this creature look cute or scary?

- How many legs does it have?

- What does it like to eat?

Sound out the words

Encourage your child to sound out the letters in any words he or she does not know. Look at the common "key" words listed at the back of the book and see which of them your child can find on each page.

Check for understanding

It is one thing to understand the meaning of individual words, but you need to make sure that your child understands the facts in the text.

- Play "find the mistake." Read the text as your child looks at the words with you, but make an obvious mistake to see if he or she catches it. Ask your child to correct you and provide the right word.

- After reading the facts, close the book and think up questions to ask your child.

- Ask your child whether a fact is true or false.

- Provide your child with three answers to a question and ask him or her to pick the correct one.

Reading activities

At the end of the book, there is a simple quiz. Ask the questions and see if your child can remember the right answers. If not, encourage him or her to look up the answers.

A dictionary page will help your child to increase his or her vocabulary and a key words page reinforces your child's knowledge of the most common words.

Ant lions

The ant lion digs a steep pit
in the sand to catch ants.
It hides at the bottom
of the pit and waits
for an ant to fall in.

pit

mandible

6

Munching mandibles

When an ant falls into the pit, the ant lion grabs it with two large mouthparts, which are called mandibles.

Look here to find out what each bug eats!

What's for dinner?	ant	other insects

Assassin bugs

The assassin bug uses venom to turn its prey's insides into liquid. It sucks the insides out through its straw-like mouth!

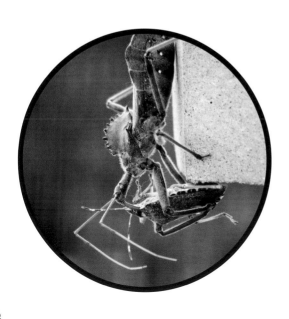

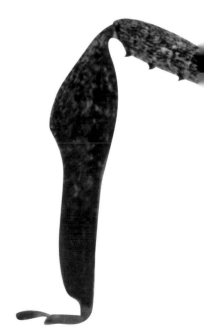

Top hunters

Assassin bugs hunt their prey in many different ways. Some also suck blood!

·······→ antenna

mouth

By covering itself in dead ants, this assassin bug can hide from attacking jumping spiders!

What's for dinner?	spider	termite

dead ants

assassin
bug

| bee  | blood ⬤ | ant  | cockroach  |

Centipedes

Some tropical centipedes are very aggressive. They kill and eat frogs, mice, snakes, birds, and even bats!

front leg

What's for dinner?	snake	small insects

Deadly legs

Centipedes stab venom into their prey using their sharp, claw-like front legs!

antenna

og | small birds | mouse | bat

Dragonflies

Dragonflies can
fly in any direction —
even backward!
They eat any insect they
can catch in the air.

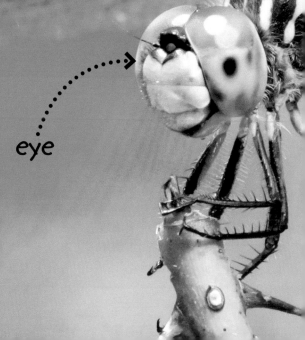

eye

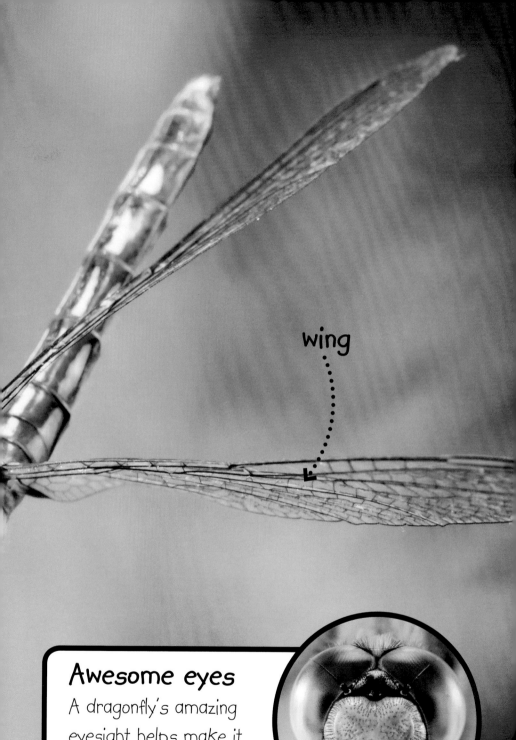

wing

Awesome eyes

A dragonfly's amazing eyesight helps make it a successful hunter.

Instead of teeth, dragonflies crunch their food with their strong, saw-like mandibles.

What's for dinner? | mosquito | fly

bee ant wasp

Giant water bugs

The giant water bug
is an underwater hunter
that can grow to
4 inches (10 cm) long!
It hunts by staying very
still and then attacking
its prey by surprise.

front leg········

What's for dinner?	tadpole	frog

Hook and hunt

The sharp hooks on a giant water bug's front legs help it to catch its prey.

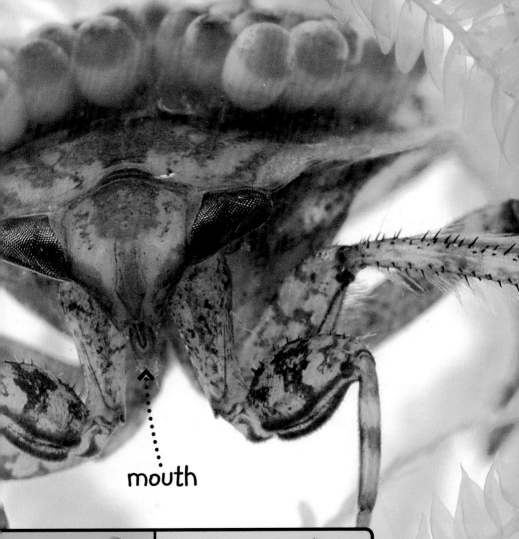

mouth

 nall fish

 salamander

Praying mantises

spiked leg

prey

A head start

Praying mantises like to eat their food alive – and they often eat the head first!

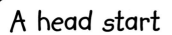

The praying mantis strikes quickly, grabbing prey with its strong, spiked legs.

What's for dinner? | cricket | fly

Some mantises look like leaves or grass. This helps them hide from prey and from enemies.

noth | caterpillar

Robber flies

Robber flies are excellent hunters and will often catch insects that are much larger than they are.

Horribly hairy

The short, stiff hairs on a robber fly's face are thought to protect its eyes from struggling prey.

| What's for dinner? | bee | fly | butterf |

24

hair

wing

| | damselfly | grasshopper |

Tiger beetles

Tiger beetles use their enormous mandibles to crush and cut their prey.

mandible

What's for dinner? fly

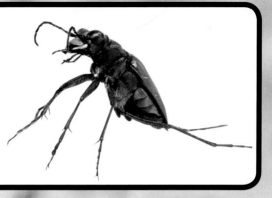

Super speedy

With a top speed of 5.6 mph (9 km/h), the tiger beetle runs fast to catch its prey!

leg

terpillar ~ grasshopper ~ spider ~

Monster meat-eater quiz

How much do you know about these monster meat eaters?

1. How fast can a tiger beetle run?

It can run at 5.6 mph (9 km/h).

2. Which bug covers itself in dead ants?

The assassin bug.

3. What does an ant lion use to grab its prey?

It uses its mandibles.

4. Who eats frogs, mice, snakes, birds, and bats?

Tropical centipedes.

5. How does a giant water bug hunt?

It stays very still and then attacks its prey by surprise.

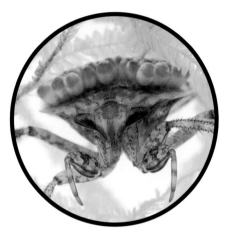

6. Which meat eater has short, stiff hairs on its face?

The robber fly.

7. How do praying mantises like to eat their food?

They like to eat their food alive and often eat the head first.

Dictionary

grab
When you grab something, you take hold of it very suddenly.

hunter
A hunter follows another animal to attack and kill it.

mandibles
Mandibles are the parts that some insects use to crush food.

prey
Prey are animals that are chased and eaten by other animals.

steep
If something is steep, it slopes up or down very sharply.

Key words

Here are some key words used in context. Help your child to use other words from the border in simple sentences.

I like to eat ants.

Dragonflies **can** fly backward.

Look at my spiked legs.

I **am** a hunter.